Ann Depta

Graphic Design by
Laura Depta Peal

Copyright © 2013 by Ann G. Depta
ISBN: 978-0-9833504-2-2

Introduction

The concepts in this book have been developed over many years of coaching leaders and working with their teams on the issues that plague every team. It is such a pleasure to watch groups go from dysfunctional to high-performing as a result of following the principles in this book. I've also observed that leaders can learn to be good coaches themselves, believing in and encouraging their teams to employ the techniques I've taught them. I think that if you apply these ideas, you will be well on your way to developing a winning team!

- Ann Depta

Praise for *A Team Leader's Alphabet*

"One of the most complex and fulfilling challenges in business can be found in leading a talented group of individuals to work as a high-performing team. With Ann's help, I used this book in a team session to help redefine commitment and direction with a group that had gotten off to a rocky start. The session helped team members appreciate individual differences and talents, get in the 'Aim Frame,' and commit to creating a set of norms. Perhaps most importantly, the book was provided to all team members and served as a common language and a reminder of what we discussed and agreed to in the session."

- D. Babst
Vice President, Client Services
Performics

"Ann Depta's latest book, *A Team Leader's Alphabet*, is a must read for everyone - whether you are an emerging leader wondering where to start or a seasoned veteran that just needs a quick refresher. As I read this book, I realized that it is more like a desk manual that I will use to 'check in' and make sure that I'm on track. It's practical, and I highly recommend reading it yourself and sharing a copy with any other leaders you know!"

- L. Hightower
Chief Operating Officer
The ABEO Group

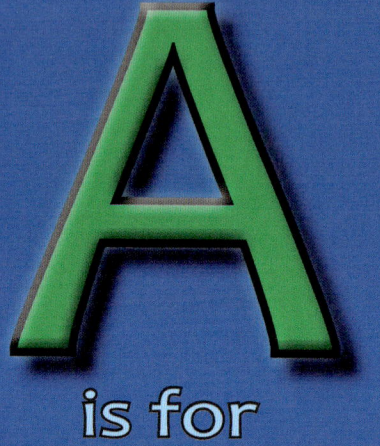

As the team *LEADER,* you're going to

HOLD
⬇
PEOPLE
⬇
ACCOUNTABLE

And you should also provide *AN ENVIRONMENT* where team members learn to hold each other *ACCOUNTABLE FOR THE PERFORMANCE OF THE WHOLE TEAM.*

find creative energy in the aim frame

B
is for
Blame Frame

Unfortunately, a large number of people in organizations expend a great deal of energy finding ways to blame others.

You and your team would be amazed at the release of creative energy if you could focus on staying in the

Aim Frame

The Aim Frame is where the team *searches for solutions,* rather than staying stuck in negative finger-pointing.

Despite the fact that most of us dislike the idea of conflict,

IT CAN BE A POSITIVE THING

IF team members understand how to deal with it.

Without constructive conflict, a team becomes susceptible to

GROUP-THINK,

and that can lead to major problems **IF NO ONE IS POINTING OUT THE FLAWS IN A STRATEGY.**

One way to encourage **constructive "conflict"** is to appoint a ***Devil's Advocate,*** who is assigned the job of poking holes in strategies and actions.

The leader of the team needs to bless this activity and *never, ever react defensively* when the DA does his or her job.

E is for Educate

Develop your people by providing educational and training opportunities.

The Team Leader

needs to develop his or her people *by providing educational and training opportunities.*

If the budget is tight, figure out creative ways to make this happen, such as *"Lunch and Learns."*

To facilitate means to make easier.

As the team leader, you don't want to do their jobs,

but you do want to find ways to *FACILITATE SUCCESSFUL OUTCOMES!*

To do this, you need to *REMOVE BARRIERS TO THEIR SUCCESS,* and you need to work with them at the skill level where they are *because everyone is different.*

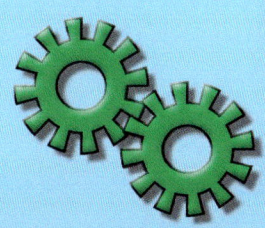

Every Team
who acts as needs a person
The Glue!

> This is someone who remembers to consider the people factor when decisions are made or actions are taken.

If you as the team leader don't find that fits your personality, make sure you have someone on the team for whom it is a fit, and appoint them to remind you.

respectful honesty

H
is for
Honesty

*respectful honesty
is the foundation of trust*

RESPECTFUL HONESTY IS THE FOUNDATION OF TRUST

ON WHICH ALL TEAM FUNCTIONING IS BUILT

respectful honesty is the foundation of trust

THUS, TEAM MEMBERS NEED TO FEEL FREE TO SAY WHAT'S ON THEIR MINDS, AS LONG AS IT'S DONE IN A WAY THAT DOESN'T ATTACK OTHERS.

Almost everybody is juggling

A
Whole
lot
of
Balls
these days.

Members of a high performing team can help each other with this issue.

There is strength in numbers

when everybody is pulling in the same direction.

This one is a no-no.

Managing a team through KITA is a sure way to destroy team effectiveness.

Nobody wants to work for a team leader who threatens and bullies team members.

A TEAM THAT HAS FUN AND CELEBRATES SUCCESS IS A HAPPY TEAM THAT WILL GIVE YOU THEIR BEST THROUGH THICK AND THIN.

PLAN SPECIAL OCCASIONS WHERE TEAM MEMBERS CAN RELAX AND LAUGH A LOT!

M is for Meetings

the lifeblood of effective teams

This is one of my favorites!

In general nobody seems to like meetings.

But meetings are the *LIFEBLOOD* of effective teams.

Think of it this way: meetings are the practice sessions for a team.

An athletic team has to have practice as a group in addition to individual skill practice.

Think scrimmage rather than one-on-one coaching.

N is for

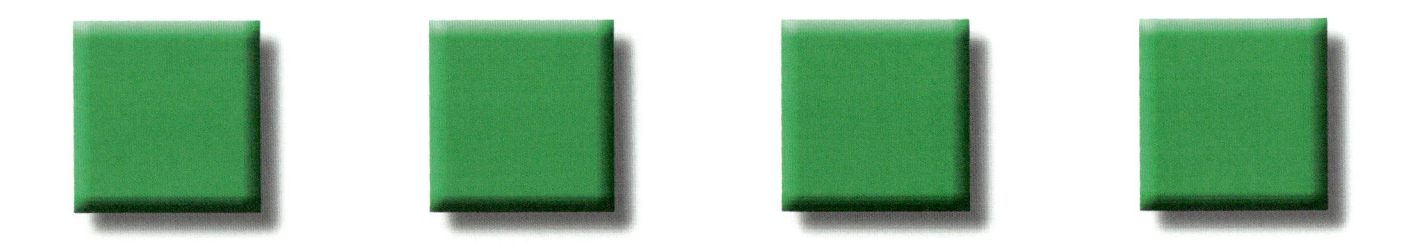

Norms

Norms are unwritten and unspoken ways in which people in a group behave.

For example, what is your group's norm for starting and ending meetings on time?

Your team needs to examine its own norms, both healthy and unhealthy

and agree to identify and abide by healthy norms. Every team needs to develop a set of Operating Agreements (making healthy group norms explicit).

This will help keep group dynamics flowing smoothly.

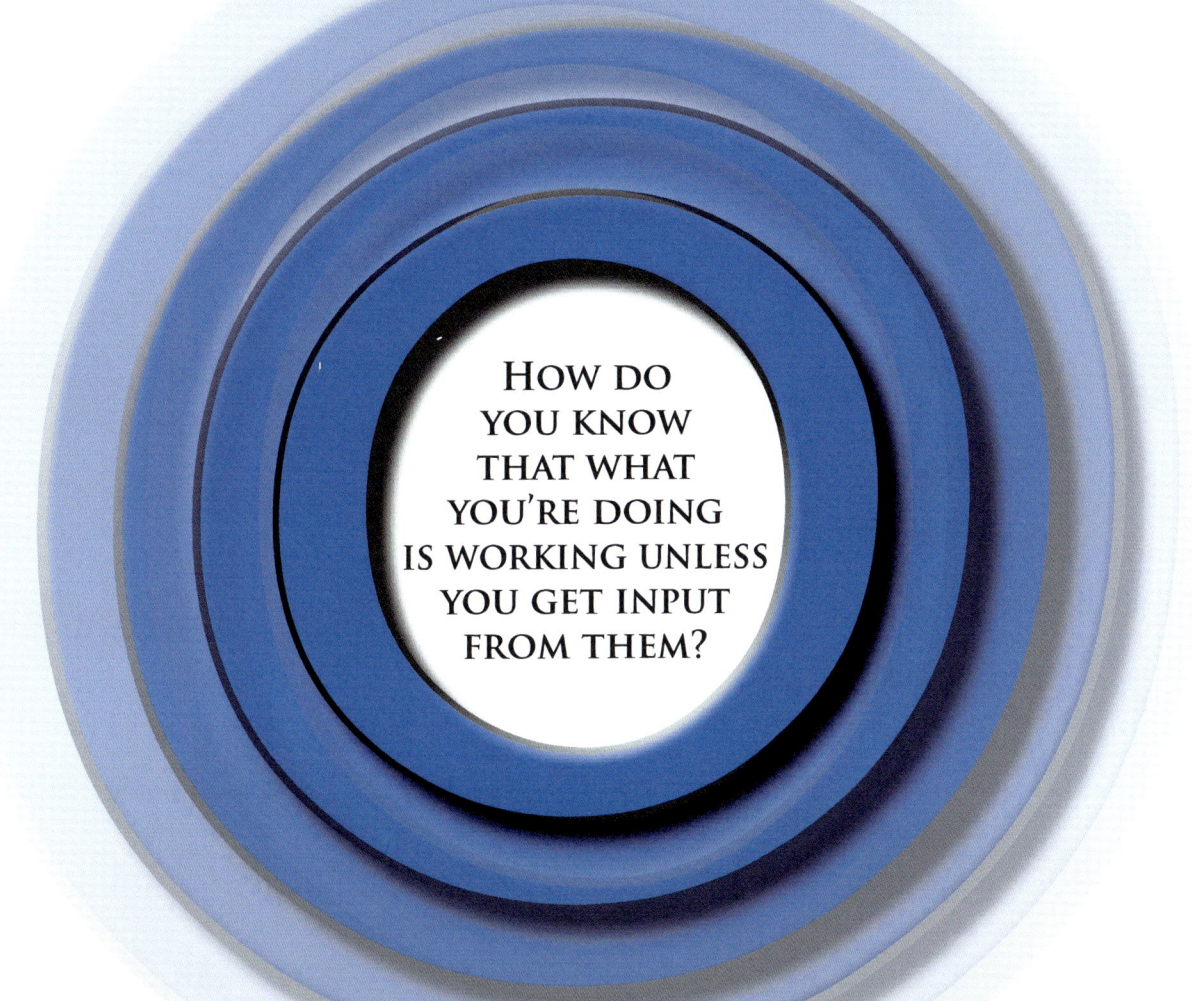

Some team leaders never solicit feedack from their team members.

How do you know that what you're doing is working unless you get input from them?

It's tricky though; you can never, ever be defensive when you receive it.

For a team to be truly effective,

members need to learn about their own and their teammates' personality styles.

Thus, every team leader needs to find a way for team members to participate in a personality assessment. There are myriad assessments that will help. My personal favorite is the DiSC Personality Profile.

If team members practice flexibility in working with others' styles, *the team will thrive!*

You and your team should be on a **QUEST FOR EXCELLENCE!**

Set expectations HIGH, but make sure people have the *TOOLS* and *INFORMATION* they need.

$$\frac{R}{e+s} \pm \left(\frac{u \times l}{t+s}\right) =$$

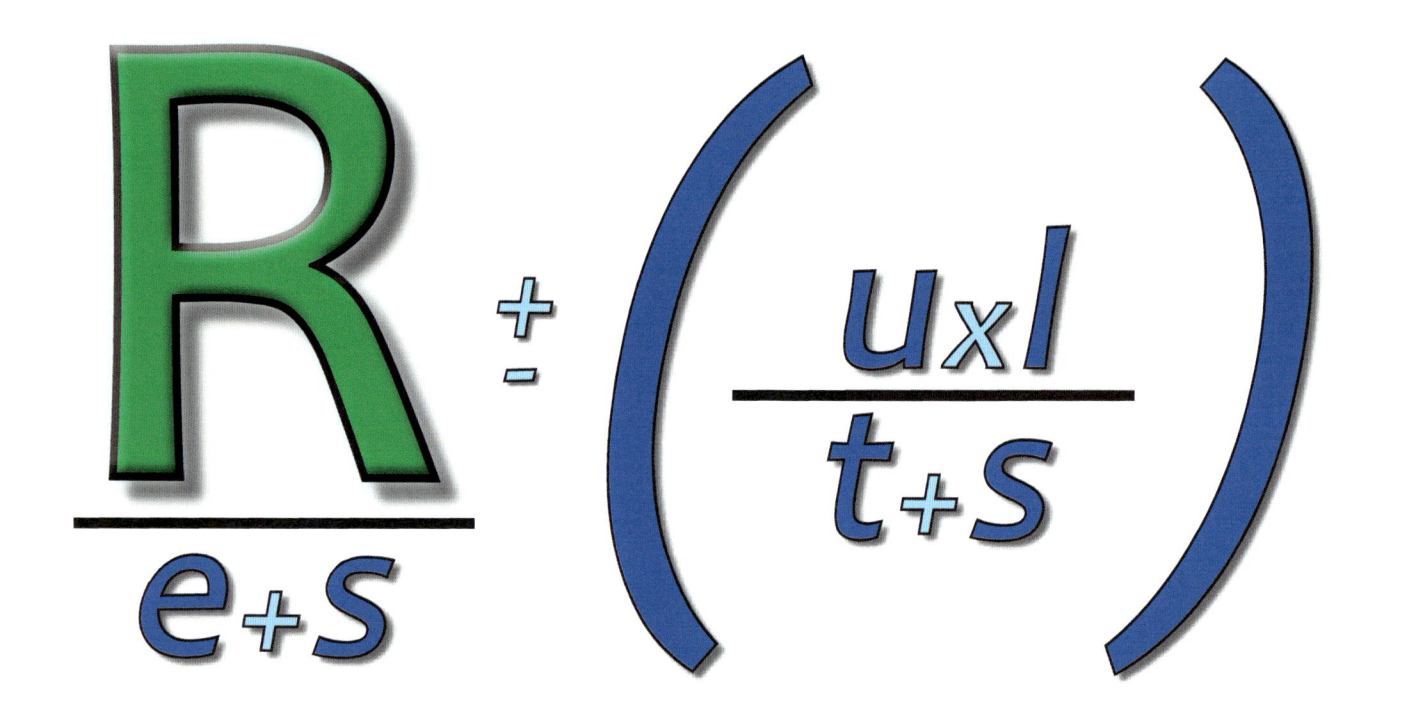

Results

$$\sqrt{\dfrac{\text{A TEAM THAT GETS ALONG WELL WITH EACH OTHER}}{\text{(AND HAS A LOT OF FUN TOO)}} \text{ IS GREAT,}}$$

BUT THAT'S NOT ALL YOU'RE THERE FOR.

A TEAM THAT DOESN'T GET RESULTS IS A LOSING TEAM.

S is for Support

team members have each other's backs

Do your team members have each other's backs?

Or are they stabbing each other's backs?

If it's the latter, they are definitely not a team.

Tolerance

A successful team leader

must develop

TOLERANCE

**for team members
who are hard-wired
differently from them.**
(See letter P for Personalities.)

Along with tolerance
comes *patience*
when people go about a task or project
differently from the way you
might do it or they work a bit
more slowly than you do.

What counts are the
results!

U is for

*free your team
and watch them thrive*

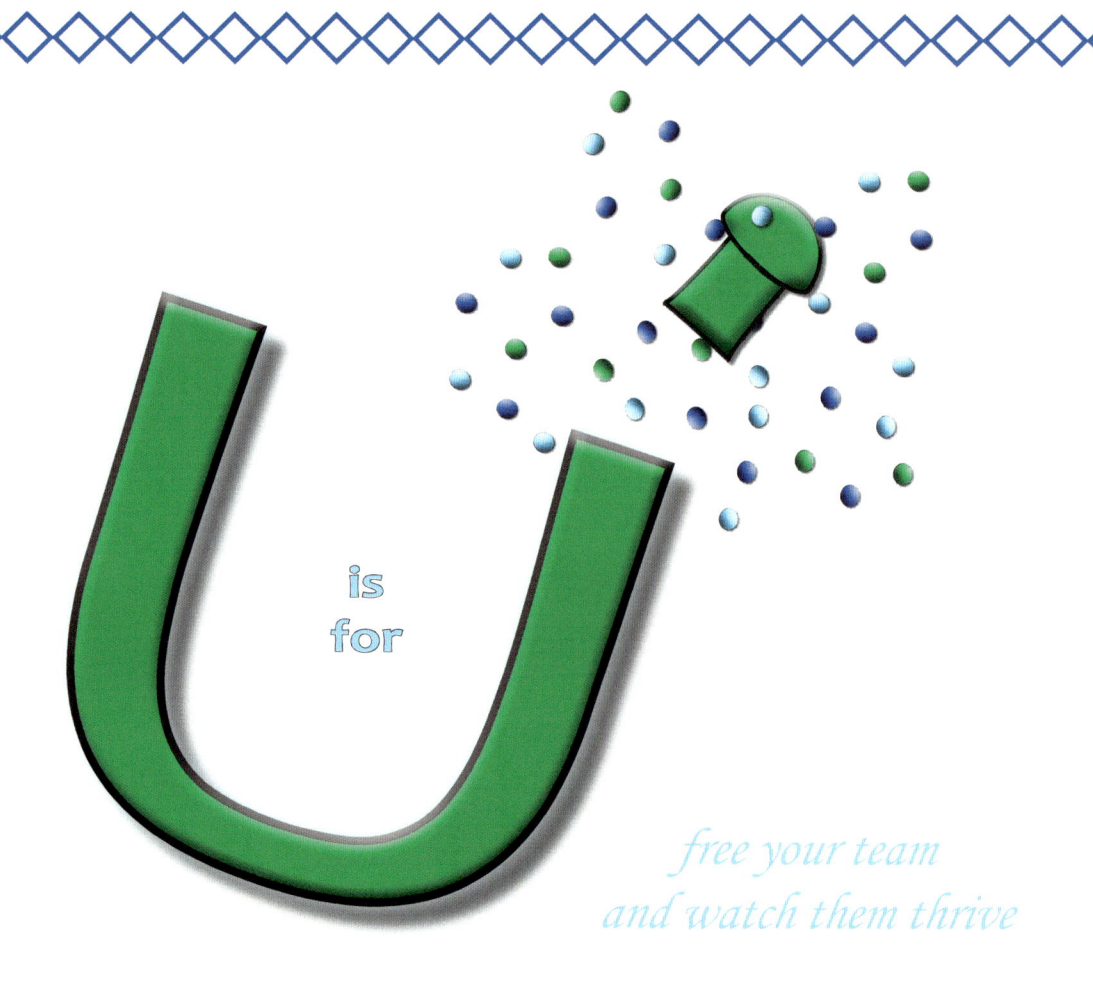

Uncork

WEBSTER SAYS
TO UNCORK MEANS

TO *FREE* FROM A CONSTRAINED STATE!

UNCORK YOUR TEAM

AND WATCH THEM THRIVE!

V is for **Venting**

It's okay to allow a team to **VENT** once in awhile, but don't let them stay in that mode. This will drag them into the **Blame Frame** (See Letter B).

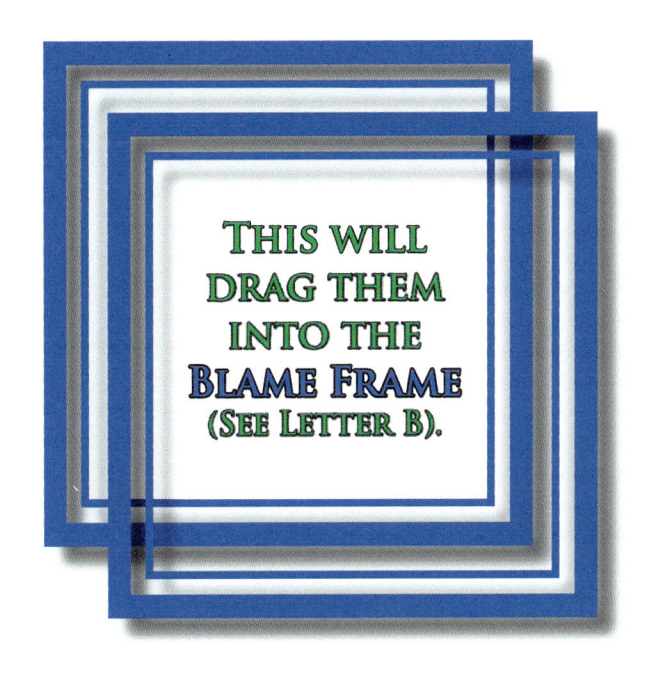

Turn them toward the **Aim Frame.**

Even batteries have negative charges, but once the team has **BRIEFLY VENTED** their negative charges,

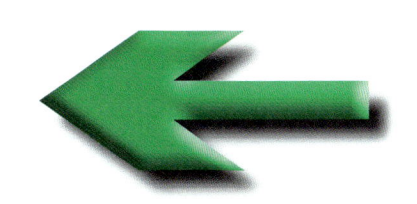

W is for Wisdom

collective wisdom

Collective Wisdom

almost always results in better decisions and actions than your own.

You may be very wise, but you are limited by your own personality style and your life history and experience.

Bring your team together to solve problems. In itself that is a teambuilding exercise.

X is for

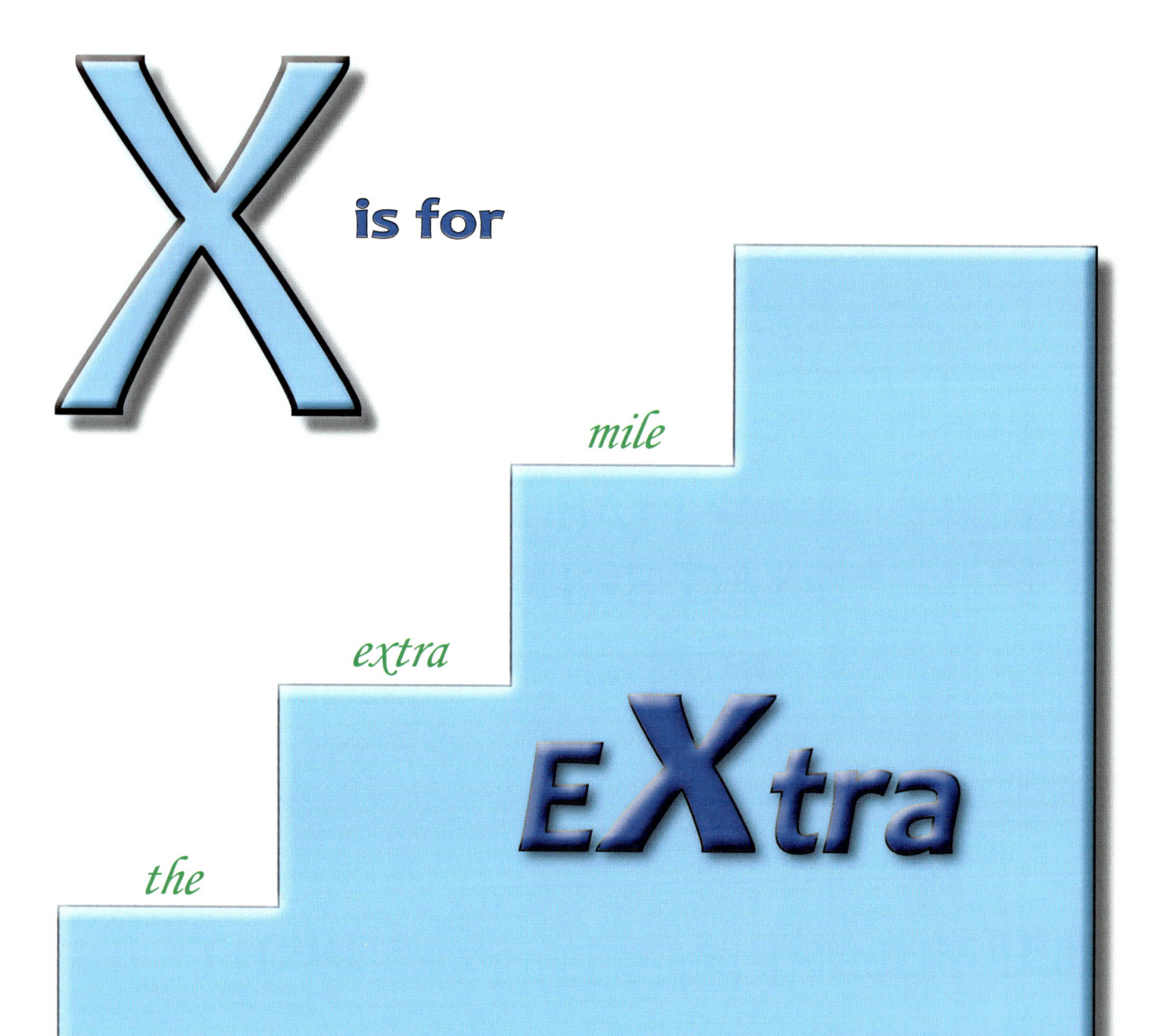

the *extra* *mile*

EXtra

LEADERS

**WHO FOLLOW
THESE PROVEN PRINCIPLES**

HAVE TEAMS WHO GO

THE EXTRA MILE

AND BECOME

TRULY HIGH-PERFORMING!

YYYYYY is for

yes *yes* *yes* *yes* *yes*

"Yes" Man
(or Woman)

The *LAST* thing you want

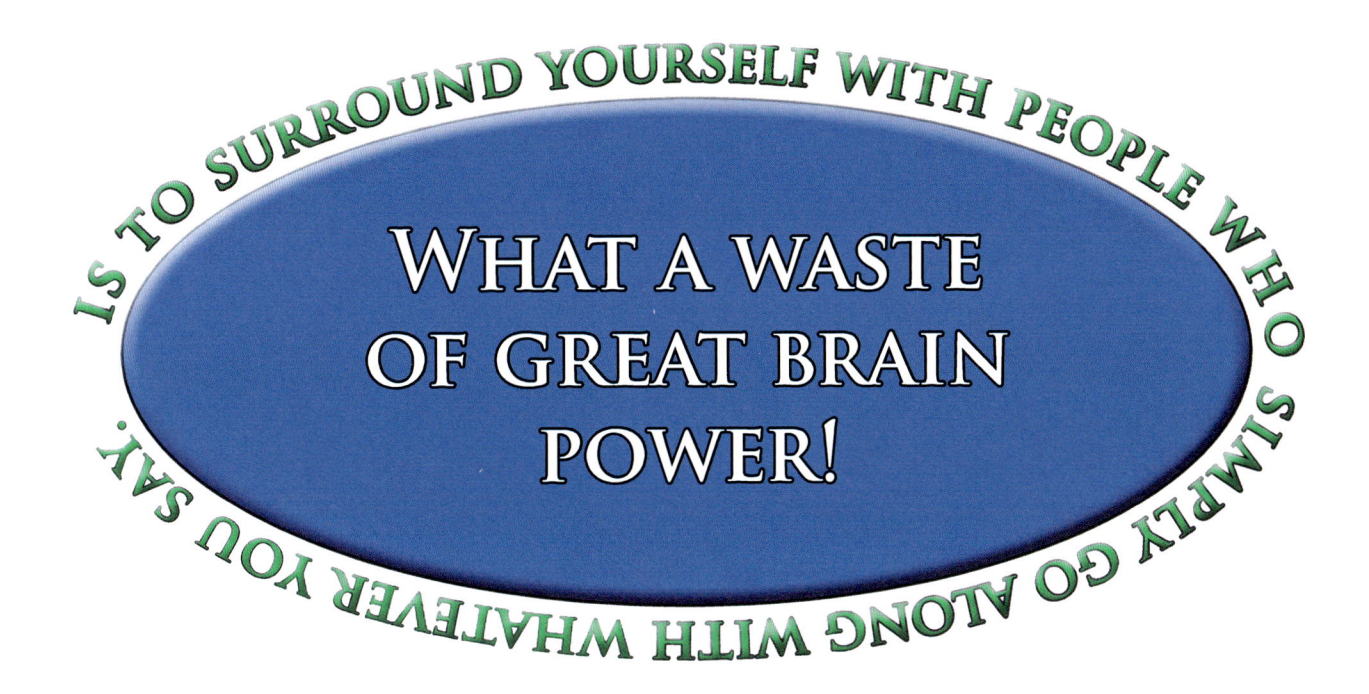

is to surround yourself with people who simply go along with whatever you say.

What a waste of great brain power!

Just to make sure that doesn't happen, appoint a
Devil's Advocate
for your team.
(See Letter D)

Z

Zoom

If you become a skilled team leader, your team will

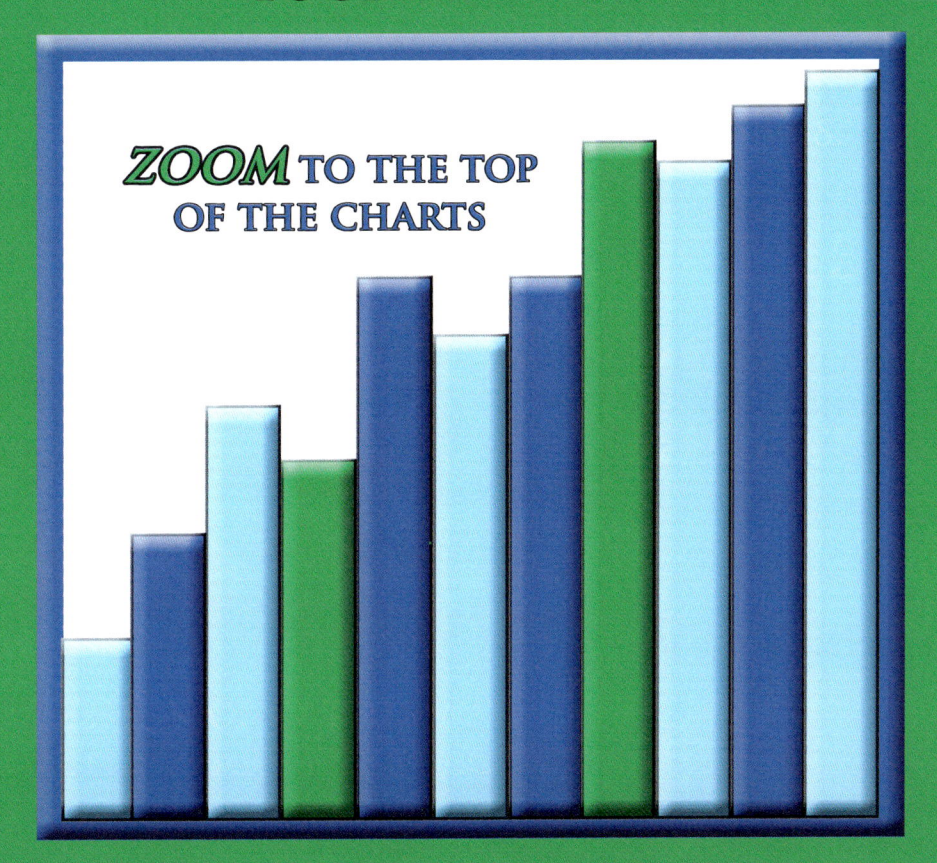

ZOOM TO THE TOP OF THE CHARTS

in productivity and exceptional deliverables.

Celebrate!!

ANN DEPTA

ABOUT THE AUTHOR

Ann Depta is passionate about all things leadership. After earning her M.A. in Instructional Systems at the University of Minnesota, she worked her way into her dream job as Vice President and Manager of Leadership Development at First Union National Bank in Charlotte. In 1990 she set a new career goal and founded Meridian Consulting Group, which allows her to coach and develop strong leaders. She continues to love and cherish her work to this day. Her other loves are her family, hiking and the arts.

Meridian Consulting Group
HELPING YOUR BUSINESS REACH ITS HIGHEST POTENTIAL

1800 CAMDEN RD, SUITE 107, #233
CHARLOTTE, NC 28203
PH (704) 376-7953
ADEPTA@MERIDIANCONSULT.COM
WWW.MERIDIANCONSULT.COM